Cash Follows the Leader

Uninterrupted Daily Growth with High Cash Value Life Insurance

Cash Follows the Leader

Uninterrupted Daily Growth with High Cash Value Life Insurance

Jayson Lowe and Richard Canfield

by Jayson Lowe and Richard Canfield

Library of Congress Cataloging-in-Publication Data has been applied for

ISBN: 978-1-7781450-0-1

Limit of Liability Disclaimer of Warranty: The material and all information related to Wealth Without Bay Street, the book series, the process of Becoming Your Own Banker®, and The Infinite Banking Concept®, printed in Wealth Without Bay Street books, posted on Wealth Without Bay Street websites, and YouTube Channel are designed to educate and provide general information regarding all subject matter covered. It is marketed and distributed with the understanding that the authors and the publishers are not engaged in rendering legal, financial, or other professional advice. It is also understood that laws and practices may vary from province to province, state to state, and are subject to change. All illustrations provided in these materials are for educational purposes only, and individual results will vary. Each illustration provided is unique to that individual, and your personal results may vary. Because each factual situation is different, specific advice should be tailored to each individual's particular circumstances. For this reason, the reader is advised to consult with qualified licensed professionals of their choosing regarding that individual's specific situation. The authors have taken reasonable precautions in the preparation of all materials and believe the facts presented are accurate as of the date it was written. However, neither the authors nor the publisher assumes any responsibility for any errors or omissions. The authors and publisher specifically disclaim any liability resulting from the use or application of the information contained in all materials, and the information is neither intended nor should be relied upon as legal, financial, or any other advice related to individual situations. The Infinite Banking Concept® is a registered trademark of Infinite Banking Concepts, LLC. Wealth Without Bay Street is independent of and is not affiliated with, sponsored by, or endorsed by Infinite Banking Concepts, LLC.

This book is dedicated to R. Nelson Nash

Cash Follows the Leader

Here's What's Inside:

ACCESS YOUR FREE GIFT!

READ THIS FIRST

As a thank you for subscribing to our book series, we're giving you a gift of access to our team and our supplemental resources so that you can start the process of Becoming Your Own Banker®, The Infinite Banking Concept®.

Your gift comes with the following:

- Connecting you with an experienced authorized Infinite Banking practitioner on our team for a conversation to answer your questions and uncover how this process is best suited for you
- A free trial account on our Client Success Portal gives you instant access to all our resources and coaching, on-demand, on any device, at your time of need.

TEXT THE WORD "SCHEDULE" TO: (844) 936 2656

wealthwithoutbaystreet.com/bonus

Foreword

Since the early 2010s, a deluge of marketing has flooded the internet—first on YouTube and then on TikTok, particularly—emphasizing the role of creatively-designed whole life insurance in financial strategy. The inspiration for virtually every instance of this strain of internet-era marketing can be traced to the teachings of the late, great R. Nelson Nash, mentor to myself and to the authors of this book.

Nelson Nash coined the term Infinite Banking Concept, or IBC for short, to encompass his financial philosophy. One of his core insights is that the fundamental financial problem confronting the average North American is a lack of control over what Nelson called "the banking function." The dominant, contemporary financial paradigm teaches us to outsource our need for capital—for credit—to Wall Street for Americans and Bay Street for Canadians. The consequence of this arrangement is, at least, two-fold: the average North American loses the interest and dividends he otherwise would have accumulated had he been the one in control of the capital required for his financing needs, and he becomes dependent on the institutions that rush to meet the need that he's been conditioned to outsource.

In his book *Becoming Your Own Banker*, published in 2000, Nelson demonstrates that by implementing the IBC, by progressively reclaiming more and more of "the banking function" through substantial premium payment to properly-designed dividend-paying whole life insurance from a mutual company, one could opt out of this unpleasant paradigm, reverse these dynamics, and trigger a systematic capital accumulation process all under the individual's own private, contractual control.

In doing so, Nelson used spreadsheet-style examples to illustrate the practical benefit of his philosophy. This "IBC method" of financing the ordinary purchases in one's life results in a substantial accumulation of cash value (i.e., equity) in whole life insurance. Nelson showed how this cash value could be used, ultimately, to provide for a substantial ongoing cash flow late in life, well in excess of the amounts paid into these policies, all in a tax-deferred, non-market-correlated environment.

Fast forward to the present day.

Spend any meaningful length of time on the internet, and one will find countless iterations of numerical depictions of whole life policy values—sometimes in the form of a partial, formal life insurance policy "illustration" document, sometimes in the form of an informal spreadsheet.

Sadly, what's often missing from these marketing materials is any mention of Nelson Nash whatsoever.

The result is something like a rudderless ship, an edifice of financial education built on a foundation of sand. The marketing material bears some superficial relation to Nelson Nash and IBC but lacks his spirit and with it, the essence of his philosophy—that counter-intuitive emphasis on this unusual idea of controlling "the banking function."

In this spiritually dry desert of internet marketing, things get transactional quickly. The focus turns abruptly, if not only, to the product—a dividend-paying whole life policy—and away from the process of reclamation of control over the banking function.

Practically speaking, the result is the proliferation of creatively designed whole life insurance policies that, at their core, will not serve the individual in the manner expected. Perhaps the most common thread linking these creatively designed policies is the idea that there should be as little base premium as possible in these ostensibly "banking-style" whole life policies.

No banker ever started a bank with the expectation of only contributing to and accumulating capital for as little time as possible.

And yet, that's exactly what is happening and what will happen with these anti-base premium policies. To conform to tax law in the US and Canada and to preserve the proper, preferable tax treatment of traditional whole life insurance, policy owners of anti-base premium policies will find themselves—sooner rather than later—in the unhappy position of dramatically throttling down their premium payments into their allegedly "banking style" policies.

This short book is a rare, gentle exception to these seemingly ubiquitous approaches.

Its core theme is a much-needed reorientation to the fundamental infrastructure of a whole life insurance policy, what in the States we call the "base policy"—the base premium and the initial death benefit associated with it.

As the housing metaphor, you'll encounter will illuminate how the base policy, and therefore the base premium, is the prerequisite foundation of a properly-designed IBC-style whole life policy. Without it or with as little of it as possible, one only handicaps his long-term potential for capital accumulation.

Yes, minimum base premium payment and maximum PUA premium payment in the first policy year does create more cash value early on in the life of these policies. But at what cost? And isn't that the prevailing current in contemporary culture: the quick fix with little to no concern for future viability?

The anti-base premium approach to whole life insurance design is an attempt to commodify the Infinite Banking Concept®, to turn whole life into what it is not: a clever alternative investment. The essence of the approach is the implicit belief that premium is a bad thing and that we should aim for as much cash value for as little premium in as little time as the life insurance company will allow. This is the opposite of what Nelson Nash taught us.

Solving for the "banking function" means pursuing and acquiring a system of policies that will permit substantial premium payment for as long as we might want the contractual right—but not the obligation—to pay. Premium payments, viewed in this light, are a good thing, and that goes for PUA and base premium. In fact, the former is only payable because of the latter.

Two of Nelson's "rules" for practicing his IBC were Think Long Range and Don't be Afraid to Capitalize. This book does the important and uncommon work of advocating for adherence to these vital guidelines when implementing Nelson's teachings.

I hope, at the very least, you'll take these ideas to heart and grant them your honest and full consideration. You may just find, as I have, that accepting them—and acting on them—will produce what Nelson called "a personal monetary system" that will accept substantial premiums for as long as you're willing and able to pay them so that—God willing—you may take back authority over the banking function in your life.

-Ryan Griggs

CEO Griggs Capital Strategies

Meet the Authors

"We believe that financial control should be in your hands, not the banks, not the government, not the stock market." – Jayson Lowe, Richard Canfield

We are Jayson Lowe and Richard Canfield, co-authors of this book series. As children, we were impacted by financial difficulties within our families, experiencing money struggles firsthand. Having now achieved cash confidence and financial control as adults, we decided to write this book series to serve as an inspiration and a guide for others to create their own peaceful, stress-free way of life financially.

It was January 2010, a cold, snowy night in Edmonton, Alberta, when we began educating individuals on our financial process inside a boardroom no bigger than a closet. And from that tiny boardroom, our program evolved into evening and weekend events, packed each time with attendees from all across Canada.

Check out our training sessions here: http://wwbstraining.com

Our educational series, live events, and webinars all emanated from the principles we learned directly from the late R. Nelson Nash, author of the # 1 bestselling book titled *Becoming Your Own Banker*. To date, Nelson's book has sold more than 500,000 copies, and it is self-published! Why? Because it works.

Get your copies of Nelson's book here: https://shop.ascendantfinancial.ca/

In 2020, we launched our podcast and named it "Wealth Without Bay Street," with the goal of becoming the # 1 financial education podcast in North America. To date, we're well on our way to achieving that.

And now, you're holding in your hands one book from a series that will open your mind to a whole new financial world.

And if you've read our introductory book, the *Canadian's Guide to Wealth Building Without Risk*, thank you. Plus, that means you know our backstory, so there is no need to repeat it. But, if you haven't read it, we highly recommend you do, as it will give you insights into who we are and how we approach building a peaceful, stress-free way of life financially.

Our focus is on helping people just like you to achieve that in your own life. We know that money will not buy happiness, but we also know that being broke won't buy you anything. Having more money and knowing how to keep that money in your family banking system can enable you to create the financial lifestyle that you want versus reacting to the one that you already have. And by getting the bankers out of your life (or the snakes and dragons, as Nelson often said), along with doing what drives you, you can live a more purposeful life. These elements are all key to a happier existence.

Most of all, we know that you will be inspired to act and follow our easy-to-implement and straightforward process. Continue reading with the understanding that knowledge can be inspiring, but it doesn't change a darn thing unless you act upon it with determination and perseverance. You've heard the saying, "How do you eat an elephant? One bite at a time." Consider the action steps we outline in this book as taking small, easy-to-digest bites of your financial elephant. Don't stop until you reach your goals. We promise to be here as your guides along the way.

To Your Best Life,

Jayson and Richard

Chapter One

Overview

Imagine walking into your local bank, and the manager is waiting to greet you. She smiles and says, "Oh, I'm so glad you're here! We've been waiting to assist you with having access to more money, on-demand, on your terms, and without sacrificing any compound interest. After all, you should be the person in a position of total control here, not us!"

The only place a scenario like the one above could ever play out is within one's imagination.

The reality, however, is much different.

The financial system has been separating you from your money since its inception. A primary focus is to convince you to deposit your money into their fund(s) and account(s) and leave it there for decades while they get to put your money to work, multiply it, and maintain control. The longer *someone else* has all your money, the more money *someone else* makes (or loses). And how do they get you to give up control of your money? They've convinced you repeatedly they can do better with it than you can. Combine that with empty promises, fees, fees, and more fees, access restrictions, and costly penalties—it all supports their objective to keep your money within their control.

It's not your fault!

This all flies in the face of how, in our first book, an Amazon bestseller, *Canadian's Guide to Wealth Building Without Risk*, we discussed maintaining control of your money as essential to financial freedom and security. So, if you haven't read our first book, we encourage you to take the opportunity to do so. However, we will summarize some basic concepts from our first book in this book as well.

It's critical that you develop a deep understanding of the power of control. Think about control in terms of driving a car. When you are behind the wheel, you decide where you go. But if you're a passenger, you'll wind up anywhere the driver takes you. This might not be a bad thing in a car, but it's not so good financially. Within the traditional banking system, all your money is always in the trunk of *someone else's* car. However, we believe your money should be in your trunk, with you as the driver—*you* should be in the position of total and absolute control.

Enter our late mentor, R. Nelson Nash, the author of a book titled, *Becoming Your Own Banker*® and the creator of The Infinite Banking Concept®.

http://wealthwithoutbaystreet.com/books

If you've heard our podcasts, watched us on YouTube, or read our book(s), then you are aware of how Nelson Nash recommends that *you* become the banker in your life, the lives of your family members, and your business, if you are a business owner.

It all begins with a clear understanding of the problem that we all face and then recognizing the solution that Nelson developed. The solution is based on a process and the way that we think about money flowing through our hands over our lifetime. To implement this process effectively, we tap into the power of one of the oldest and most stable financial tools on planet earth. This tool is a **dividend-paying, participating whole life insurance policy, or system of**

policies, ideally with a mutual insurer, placing you in the driver's seat as a co-owner of the life insurance company.

Yes, this powerful tool can put you in the driver's seat, where you control how you go about financing the things you need throughout life, such as investments, homes, commercial property, vehicles, appliances, business equipment, and personal/business overhead. And we're not describing the use of a single policy. On the contrary, when you implement this process in your own life, you will build up a system of policies incrementally and gradually over a period of time (years). And each policy in your system will be used to further control the banking function as it relates to both you and your family's needs.

Here's a crash course on the basic components of the tool. A dividend-paying, participating whole-life policy accumulates both total cash value and total death benefit. Both components rise throughout the lifetime of the policy. The total cash value increases daily, and the total death benefit increases with each premium used to purchase paid-up insurance, which includes annual dividends.

When you initiate your first policy with one of our advisors, your policy will be engineered for a minimum premium plus (+) a flexible/optional premium amount. The minimum is the amount that you are contractually obligated to and is required to keep your base policy in force. The flexible/optional premium is what you have the contractual ***authority*** to deposit, but you're not contractually ***obligated*** to deposit. Think of the optional premium as a "rocket-booster" that rapidly accelerates both the total death benefit and total cash value while also creating a compounding effect. We will show you in this book how this powerful combination creates an ever-increasing pool of financial value that is leverageable by you, on-demand, and on your terms, all without interrupting any of the daily cash value growth.

Sounds great, right?

What does this mean for you, and how is this *product* in line with the *process* of Becoming Your Own Banker®?

Here's a scenario. You need to buy a new car. The one you want has a purchase price of $30,000. You don't just have $30,000 sitting in your checking account at the bank on Main Street. And so, like most people, you contemplate financing through the car dealer or through someone else's bank, focusing on trying to negotiate the best interest rate and repayment terms relative to your credit history.

Who's in a position of total control? It's not you! So, let's pump the BRAKES right here, so to speak, and change the scenario.

You now have a dividend-paying participating whole life policy with a total cash value of $35,000, which is rising daily. Your policy has a guaranteed loan provision, and you are a co-owner of the life insurance company. That means you can **borrow against** (not from) your total cash value at any time, on-demand, and on your terms. There are no credit checks, no income verification, no negotiating, and no hassles. You simply request a policy loan, receive $30,000 of the life insurance company's money, and a lien is placed on your total death benefit for the loan balance. $35,000 is still your total cash value amount inside your policy, and it will be higher tomorrow and every day thereafter.

You can then take the cash (policy loan proceeds) to the car dealer and negotiate a cash offer discount, then drive away with a brand-new car. At that point, you will own the car free and clear. And the policy loan is private, meaning it's not reported to Equifax or TransUnion.

Who's in a position of total control now? That's right, you are!

Now, you might find yourself thinking, *Wait a minute, would the bank I deal with now ever offer me that same deal and give me full autonomy over the repayment schedule?* Not a chance.

Do you have to pay your policy loan back? The simple answer is that eventually, it will be paid back, either while you're alive on your terms or when you die. However, having the control to make that decision also means having the responsibility to make the right choice. We'll always recommend that you repay your policy loans because that is the responsible choice and the best way to save money. In order to implement "The Infinite Banking Concept®" the way it is intended, you will want to repay so you can use the money again and again to finance all the things you will need in life.

Nelson Nash clearly stated:

"Your need for finance throughout your lifetime is far greater than your need for the death benefit. If you solve for this need through the use of dividend-paying whole life insurance, you will end up with more death benefit than you could ever get past the underwriters!"

The choice is yours. If you experience financial difficulty and cannot repay a policy loan balance, or you simply choose to not repay while you're alive, simple interest will continue to accrue and compound at each policy anniversary date. And when you die, the total loan balance will be deducted from the total death benefit. It's that simple.

Everything begins with the way that we think. Presently, all of your money flows through the books of someone else's bank, and when you are approved for a bank loan, you intend to repay it because you recognize the consequences of default (asset seizure, bad credit, judgments, wages garnished, etc.). And so, you won't think twice about replenishing your own system because you recognize the advantages of being in a position of control.

Every policy loan repayment is immediately applied to the principal balance of the loan and becomes instantly re-accessible to you. And when you are using this process to create a "family banking system," paying your loans back is a logical step to rebuilding your aquarium of money. The life insurance company also benefits. Think about it. If you are a co-owner of a business that is required to share its profits with you each and every year, where do you want your money, your financial energy flowing to? Do you want that financial energy directed to a 3rd party lender who has no incentive to grow profits on your behalf or to keep it within a closed-loop aquarium where all participating owners mutually benefit?

Does this sound better than the corner bank you currently deal with? Yes, we thought so.

What you need to know about a dividend-paying participating whole life policy:

- You maintain complete control over your hard-earned money.
- You can borrow against 90% of your total cash value on-demand, on your terms, with no questions asked.

- Your pool of financial value grows every single day, and it cannot go down.
- Policy loans do not interrupt the daily accumulation of your total cash value.
- Each year that a dividend is declared by the life insurance company, it is contractually guaranteed to be paid to you, it cannot be repossessed, and it cannot ever lose value.
- If your policy is with a mutual life company (most recommended), you participate in the divisible surplus generated from all lines of business, and the life company is responsive only to you and all other participating policy owners. There are no stockholders to share profits with or to influence the company's primary mandate.
- You create an instant tax-free estate. When optimized by one of our advisors, your death benefit steadily increases year over year with no increase in premium ever.
- Your total cash value (rising daily) is contractually guaranteed to match your total death benefit (rising monthly or annually) by age 100 of the life insured.
- Your policy is a **private unilateral contract**. It is between you and the life company and does not show up on a public registry, nor is it searchable. No one can pull the title to it. It is bound by the law of contracts and is your private property.
- This is not a get-rich-quick mechanism or investment strategy of any kind. Rather this is all about *how* you will finance the things you need in life, which can certainly include investments. It will be the only asset on your personal or business balance sheet that you can never pay into more than what it will pay out.

Nelson Nash taught us there are four characters in the "financial play."

1. Depositor
2. Borrower
3. Banker
4. Bank Owner

Presently, you are the depositor and the borrower. Someone and some organization(s) are playing the roles of the "banker" and the "bank owner" in your life right now. By implementing this process, all four characters would become *YOU*!

When you implement the process of Becoming Your Own Banker®, you become "the depositor" who is earning money and putting deposits into your own system. You become "the borrower" who needs access to money to buy the things you need in life, like the $30,000 car. You now become "the banker" who calls the shots for repaying loans, including the payment amount, frequency, total interest, and timeframe. You also become the fourth character, "the bank owner," the one who makes the most money (understandably so). This is also the character who earns a share of the profits each year from the banking business performed by all the customers of the bank. The same applies to the life insurance company that you co-own. Let that sink in. You will share in profits from *all the customers* of the life insurance company. If you are like us, you also want your friends and family members to do as much of their business within your family banking system so that everyone prospers.

When you follow the process defined in Nelson's book *Becoming Your Own Banker*, the money in your aquarium just keeps growing and never leaves your control. Contrast that with continuing to do what you're doing now financially. When you request a loan from a financial institution, such as your bank, every payment is a permanent transfer of money away from you and every generation that comes after you. For example, if you pay directly from your savings account (assuming you have the cash available), the money goes out, and your cash balance decreases. Essentially, you lose the opportunity to earn interest on that money permanently. Someone else is getting wealthy on the use and control of your money. Otherwise, the banking business wouldn't exist!

Your payments are someone else's passive income. Read that again!

The choice is obvious.

We know, and you should know, that you can and should become your own banker.

Now that we've covered those basics, let's get to the core of what this book is about. What do we mean when we say, "*cash follows the leader*"?

As we stated previously, a dividend-paying participating whole life policy has two linked components, total cash value, and total death benefit. Both grow over time on a foundation of contractual guarantees. How they grow and how that growth benefits you during your lifetime is our focus in this book.

By contract, the total cash value must equal the total death benefit by age 100 of the life that is insured in Canada (age 121 in the USA). From day one of the policy, the total death benefit is much larger than the total cash value. Based on the contractual guarantee, that total cash value *must* begin accumulating daily so that it eventually equals the total death benefit. Hence the term "cash follows the leader"!

The leader is the total death benefit; the more you grow it, the more cash value you control. Best of all, you don't have to die to WIN!

Policies vs. Policy

The late R. Nelson Nash explained that Infinite Banking involves a series or system of cash value-accumulating policies, not just one. Think of it in terms of your own bank. Is there only one branch office for your current bank? We would suspect not. The more the bank grows, the greater the need for additional branches. You will find this to be true as you look to expand the size of your own warehouse of wealth. Each time that you add another policy into your system, think of it as adding a branch office to your own family bank.

As a side note, consider assigning a name to your own banking system when you begin this process. Families that have fun with the process tend to be more open about it, and it eases the discussions with other family members as they embrace the process. For example, Nelson and his wife Mary had, at one time, 49 policies on several people's lives, including their children, grandchildren, great-grandchildren, and former business partners. Some of these individuals even had multiple policies on Nelson and Mary. These policies were all the "branch offices" of what Nelson named "The First Nash Family Bank." As of 2022, Nelson's son-in-law and president of The Nelson Nash Institute, David Stearns, has built a system of 26 family policies and is still growing. This includes their children and grandchildren and will expand to great-grandchildren, just as Nelson Nash had done.

During Nelson's lifetime, they even transferred the cash values to the next generations by changing the ownership of the policies. Yes, you can do that! In fact, Nelson indicated that he and his wife Mary had shared over $750,000 in cash values during his lifetime by transferring policies he owned to his children and grandchildren tax efficiently. These policies give you the flexibility to provide those you love with something before you pass, to experience the impact it has in their lives, as well as the joy in giving. This is just another example of that "control" we talked about, which is so important.

When Nelson passed away in March of 2019, there were 17 tax-free death benefit cheques cut by insurance companies, and Nelson left 28 cash-producing assets still in force to the next generation as part of his legacy. All of these policies will continue to grow uninterrupted. Why is that? Quite simply, because of the name of this book, *Cash Follows the Leader*, where the leader is the death benefit. Each of the 28 policies remaining is on a person that is still alive. And each year, as the death benefit rises, the available cash value must contractually grow to catch up to it!

Nelson began with policies on his own life. As a prudent businessman, from time to time, he would joint venture with other partners in various real estate projects. He recognized that if those people passed away prematurely, it would trigger a significant financial loss for Nelson and their partnership. It is common for companies and banks to take out life insurance policies on their key people for that reason. There is certainly an emotional loss, but the policy is there to compensate for a financial loss. Nelson purchased and funded policies on the lives of his joint venture partners as a means of building what he named his "warehouse of wealth" that he controlled.

On one policy, Nelson started on the life of a JV partner; the tax-free death benefit had grown to approximately $250,000 over the years he owned the policy. Nelson had used a large portion of the cash value as collateral for policy loans and utilized the proceeds to pay off his creditors from the recession of the early 1980s. Sadly, the partner passed away several years after their joint venture had ended. At the time of the partner's passing, there was an outstanding policy loan balance (principal plus interest) of $48,000. That entire policy loan balance was repaid immediately with the proceeds of the death benefit, and the remaining $202,000 was paid to Nelson, income tax-free.

Nelson did not purchase this policy for a death benefit. He purchased it as a place where he could put premium deposits to build up capital that never left his control. He borrowed against the daily cash value growth to get rid of creditors ("the snakes and dragons," as Nelson would say), one at a time, in combination with the other policies he had under his control.

For the timeframe the policy was in force, Nelson had only contributed $47,000 in total premium deposits!

Nelson was already well on his way to accomplishing his objective of taking control of the banking function in his life, using policy loans to pay off his creditors, when this “windfall” event happened. When Nelson shared this story with others, he always said: “Didn’t that (windfall of $202,000) cancel out a lot of financial mistakes I made in life? I did not buy that policy for the death benefit, but these things do happen. I bought it as a place I could store money so I could get rid of the snakes and dragons.”

It is important to understand that Nelson’s warehouse of wealth was not built overnight, and yours won’t be either. As his cash flow increased, Nelson was *intentional* about saving money and placed any new funds strategically into new policies as he was able. Time and dedication are key factors in creating and growing your own banking system, but the result of this effort creates a peaceful, stress-free way of life financially.

Picture a day when you’re living a peaceful, stress-free way of life financially. How does that make you feel?

We use the word *intentionally* and emphasize it because it takes dedication and perseverance to create and maintain. Dedication and perseverance are the by-products of intentionality. When you do anything with intention, you do it for a reason; you are focused. And let us tell you, you need to be focused and purposeful when dealing with your finances.

For example, have you ever heard about Parkinson’s law? Well, it states that “Expenses will rise to meet your income.” It’s a common occurrence where you get more money coming in, such as a pay raise or tax refund; your spending habits rise, gobble it all up, and unfortunately, for many Canadians, the more income you make, the less diligent you are on how you spend it. And despite the commonality of this phenomenon, it can be the great killer of cash flow necessary to create your family banking system.

So again, how do you become intentional about your finances? You monitor your free cash flow! First, let’s define free cash flow. Money comes in and goes out. That's cash flow. You earn an income and pay for the expenses needed to live your life. Free cash flow is the money not earmarked for specific regular bills. It's the extra or surplus, if you will, that is all too easy to squander. It is these funds that will be used to kick-start your family banking system and provide for a financially secure future.

By embracing the learning process and working with an authorized Infinite Banking practitioner on our team, you will actually "practice" the steps of being your own banker. By staying connected and active with your ongoing mentorship, you will begin to see ways to naturally increase the size of your program as you go. It has worked for us, and we both actively continue to expand our own personal systems.

Summary

As you picture this happening in your life, you will be purpose-driven to get it going. We've both done it personally, and it's been a game-changer within our families. As of the time this book is written, Jayson is adding policy number sixty-seven into his family banking system, which includes multiple policies on himself, his wife, his 4 children, extended family members, and several business partners in the Lowe Family Group of Companies. One of these policies is even on the life of Richard!

Nelson Nash taught us to think about the word diversification as "diversifying in lives insured" as we build our warehouse of wealth.

Richard has just added three new policies (a third on his wife and 2 new ones on his young children), bringing him to 13.

It all began with one policy, and then we applied the same mindsets and actions we are sharing with you to expand our system. The first step is for you to desire change and commit to action. Our subsequent chapters will detail how you perform each step toward your goal. We will be with you throughout the entire process!

So, join us, and let's put you in the driver's seat of your financial future now!

https://wealthwithoutbaystreet.com/15mincall

Chapter Two

The Foundation Is the Base Policy

Picture your home's foundation as we describe the importance of the base policy. And just as a foundation's primary purpose is to hold your house up, the base policy also needs to be built right the first time. The following elements will make your base policy structurally sound:

- The policy owner (you) outranks everybody.
- The minimum required premium you choose to deposit can never increase; it can go down but never up.
- You have ready access to money on-demand, on your terms, by utilizing the guaranteed policy loan provision.
- You co-own the lender (the life insurance company).
- When you access policy loan(s), you control the repayment schedule (remember the characters in the financial play).
- The eventual payment of death benefit proceeds is contractually guaranteed and income tax-free to your named beneficiary(s).
- Your total cash value rises daily and cannot go backward, and there is no taxation on the daily accrual.
- Each year that a dividend is declared by the life company you co-own, it is contractually guaranteed to be paid, cannot be repossessed, cannot lose value, and does not trigger tax when used to purchase paid-up additions.

All the above and more make up the foundation of your system. In simplicity, we're dealing with a life insurance contract, a policy, or a system of policies. This unilateral binding contract has two essential building blocks: total cash value and total death benefit. By age 100 of the life insured, both components must match.

Shifting our thinking from the product (the policy) back to the process (Becoming Your Own Banker®), a bank requires deposits in order to make loans. And regardless of whether or not you become the banker in your life as it relates to your needs, the truth is you are always going to need the use of money.

And that money must come from somewhere and some organization. You can become that someone, and the life insurance company that you co-own can become that organization. In this way, you now share in the profits of the lending business that you require for your life's needs, plus the lending needs of others who conduct their financial affairs this way.

Think of total cash value as your own aquarium of capital that can (and should) flow at a cost to meet your and other family members' needs. Think of your pool of financial value being utilized as collateral to borrow against on your terms, for your family and your business, and to purchase all the things that you need throughout your lifetime. And because your aquarium grows daily, the percentage (%) of the banking function that you can control in your life also grows daily.

Isn't that good?

As time progresses, your system of policies becomes your indestructible warehouse of wealth. And gradually, what you would've previously utilized *someone else's bank* for, you begin to finance through your own family banking system. It all boils down to WHERE the money is flowing to and WHO that money is being put to work for.

You do have options. You can keep working hard and have all your income continue flowing through the books of someone else's bank, or you can incrementally create your own system and take over the banking function as it relates to your needs. It all boils down to logic and motivation. Is it logical to become a banker in your life? And are you motivated to take action?

https://wealthwithoutbaystreet.com/15mincall

I want to take you back to the four characters in the financial play as we review another example. Suppose your daughter needs access to money for this semester's college tuition. She comes to "the bank of Mom and Dad," asking for $15,000. You look inside your system of policies and see cash values available greater than $15,000.

Can you simply request a policy loan and then write your daughter a cheque? Yes, that is your privilege. But that is not taking control of the banking function as it relates to this particular need.

On the other hand, to properly implement the process and to build a sound "family banking system," you draft a loan agreement that includes a predetermined repayment schedule, you review that agreement with your daughter in its entirety, and then all parties sign off prior to the release of funds.

Who are the 4 characters in this example?

- The Depositor - **You**
- The Borrower - **Your Daughter**
- The Banker - **You**
- The Bank Owner - **You**

As the "banker" and the "bank owner," you will earn interest on the amount borrowed while still accumulating more total cash value inside of your system every single day. Remember, your total cash value amount increases with premium deposits and has contractually guaranteed daily growth; it must do this to follow the leader (total death benefit) to age 100. Your cash value does NOT go down whenever a policy loan is accessed. Best of all, when you transfer the knowledge of the process along with the money, your daughter will know that every dollar she pays back into the family banking system will be available to her again and again and again throughout her own lifetime.

Designing the Base Policy to Meet Your Needs

The one thing we can say for certain is that no two policies are alike. Why? Well, no two people are alike, and everyone's needs vary. As you picture what it will be like working with an advisor on our team to create your own base policy, we also want you to think about how you'll feel when you're in a position of control.

Picture a day when you're in a position of total and absolute control financially.

In designing your policy or system of policies, our team will focus on consideration for your needs and core objectives, both while you're alive and when that day comes, and you've passed away.

We will help you to prepare for each step in an upcoming chapter.

Adding Floors to Your Financial House with Paid-Up Additions (PUA)

Just as the foundation supports your home and bears the weight, the same applies to your base policy. In this segment, we'll add floors to your financial house that will all stack on top of the foundation. We'll refer to each floor as a paid-up addition or simply as a "PUA."

What are they, and how do they work?

A paid-up addition (PUA) is an add-on to your base policy and is stacked on top of one another, just like the floors of your home. There are two ways to buy paid-up additions:

- Premium payments.
- Using your annual dividends.

When your policy is designed, you'll recall a portion of the total premium is flexible or optional. This optional portion, when paid, immediately buys a paid-up addition. If you're paying a premium monthly, a paid-up addition is also purchased monthly. If you pay your premium annually, a paid-up addition is also purchased annually. In most cases, the policy owner can contribute this optional premium on a flexible (ad hoc) basis during the policy year up to a predetermined maximum amount.

Because you are the policy owner, you decide what happens with your dividends. You can and should select "paid-up additions" as your dividend election. Each year that a dividend is declared, it will be used to purchase even more paid-up additions. And each paid-up addition also receives a dividend every year that dividends are declared in the future. The compounding effect that you create inside of your policy can become enormous!

What does each paid-up addition premium buy? More participating whole-life death benefit which must also accumulate its equivalent in cash value. The PUA is a single premium whole-life policy added on top of the existing foundation of the base policy.

For example, you have a foundation and a starting base policy death benefit of $500,000. You purchase a paid-up addition of $50,000 in additional death benefits creating a new total death benefit. The total death benefit is now $550,000. Now, because the total cash value is guaranteed to match the total death benefit, the daily growth accelerates because the life-insured is aging closer to 100. With each new floor added, the rate of cash value growth must speed up to chase after it.

Once acquired, this increase in total death benefit is locked in. It is appropriately named "paid-up" because it's paid for and essentially becomes an increase to the guarantee of the contract. This means the policy owner's behavior of purchasing paid-up additions has created a permanent advantage.

Let's expand:

Kim and Jack are a married couple. They decide to insure Jack, age 35, as the primary income earner. They purchase a dividend-paying participating whole life insurance policy with a starting death benefit that has merit, meaning it's needed. They want to have the *option* of depositing a maximum of $15,000 each year but only be *contractually obligated* to deposit a minimum of $5,000 each year. This total amount is both comfortable and affordable for them. The amount that you choose will obviously be different from Kim and Jack's as your situation and needs will be different. However, we always recommend that your policy with paid-up additions satisfies the same criteria of comfort and affordability.

So, back to our example, the base policy requires a minimum premium of $5,000 annually. Kim and Jack spend less money than what they earn and agree they want to continue saving their disposable income ($10,000+) and simply change where that money resides. Working with the right advisor on our team, the policy was engineered to warehouse that additional $10,000.

In other words, Kim and Jack now have *the contractual authority* (control) to deposit more than $5,000 to a maximum of $15,000 in any given year, but they're not *contractually obligated* to deposit anything more than $5,000, giving them desired flexibility.

Kim and Jack's advisor explains the policy is a product, whereas "Becoming Your Own Banker®" is a process. Furthermore, they understand that their money must reside somewhere.

Kim and Jack value the coaching they receive and prioritize depositing a total of $15,000 into their policy as often as possible. The optional amount of $10,000 immediately purchases a large paid-up addition, a floor, that is stacked onto the base policy. And each year, they repeat that the total death benefit increases, so the total cash value must follow. Because they co-own the life insurance company, the determination of the dividend amount paid to them each year is based primarily on "the contribution principle." Each premium deposit increases their policy's contribution to the net earnings of the life insurance company, thereby increasing their share of the divisible surplus. Each year dividends are declared; they are paid on the base policy *AND* every paid-up addition. This powerful compounding effect is created by Kim and Jack.

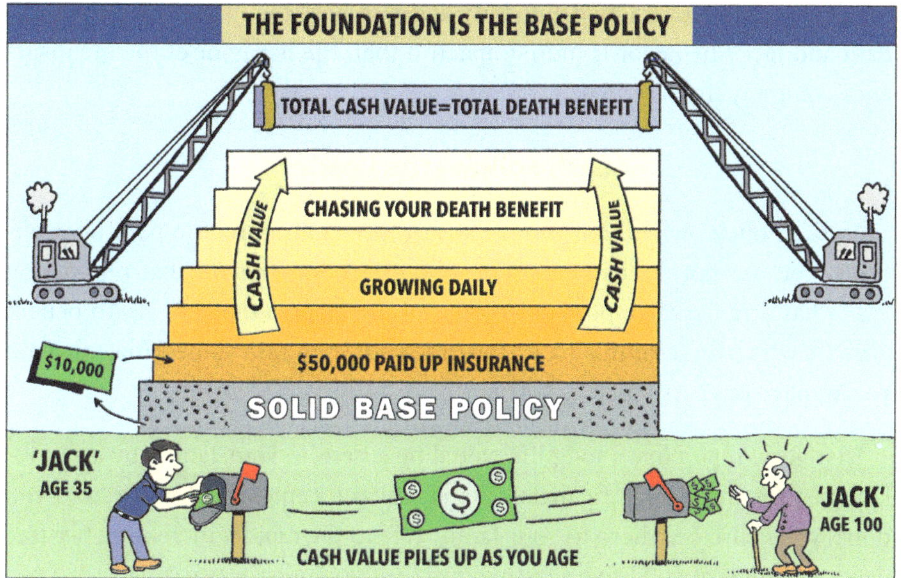

This reminds us of something Nelson often said, ***"The policy owner's behavior is far more critical than the behavior of the life insurance company."***

Please read that again.

Then let's recap what we've discussed on paid-up additions:

- They are basically single premium "paid-up" whole-life policies that are stacked on top of one another.
- Creates an immediate increase in total cash value and total death benefit.
- Creates an unstoppable accumulation of new cash values to equal the newly increased paid-up death benefit.
- Increases all future cumulative dividends.

By acquiring paid-up additions, Kim and Jack create a ripple effect with their money. For example, think of how a tree grows each year. A new layer is added to the outside of each growing season. We refer to this as the rings of the tree. Each ring represents a year of uninterrupted growth. This same principle happens with the whole life policy. With the power of paid-up additions every year, the circumference of the policy increases, and each annual dividend is paid on an ever-increasing circumference. And for each subsequent year, the dividends will build on the years before and so on. This impact is based on their decision to exercise their contractual authority and purchase the PUA. In other words, Kim and Jack's behavior is more impactful than the behavior of the life insurance company they co-own.

Cash Follows the Leader

As the policy owner, you possess the authority to purchase paid-up additions. You are not obligated to. That is control. Understand that purchasing PUAs has a remarkable positive and lasting impact on the total death benefit growth, which forces immediate growth of your total cash value. How much do you want to buy? As much as you can!

Therefore, if you live a long life, you'll be a hero to your family by accumulating a growing pool of financial capital that you can use as you see fit. If you don't, you'll also be a hero to your family due to the rapidly increasing tax-free death benefit that will leave a lasting impact if you pass away early.

It's a financially good situation either way.

Let's look at Kim and Jack's example from a slightly different vantage point.

When Kim and Jack use $10,000 of their disposable income to buy paid-up additions, they simultaneously add on the death benefit, which is far more than the $10,000 they put in. Respecting their privacy, we'll use arbitrary numbers to highlight this point. For example, their policy had a starting death benefit of $500,000. In exchange for the $10,000 voluntary premium payment, they purchase $50,000 of the PUA death benefit. The total death benefit is now $550,000. Again, a one-time payment meant they now have a lump sum additional death benefit instantly. They will never be required to pay any future premium for this newly acquired $50,000 death benefit. The insurance company is contractually obligated to grow the total cash value asset that Kim and Jack control to equal the total cumulative death benefit (which will continue to increase with every new PUA premium and dividends added). In essence, they have traded $10,000 today for $50,000 of stable, lifelong cash growth without market risk and guaranteed payment upon death. A substantial amount of this is readily available as collateral via a policy loan immediately. As this value grows each year, they will accumulate an ever-increasing total cash value that can be used strategically as collateral to achieve their lifelong purchasing needs and investing opportunities.

How Is It Possible?

A question often asked is, how is it possible? Why would the life insurance company provide this? Is it a coincidence that through all the major financial events we've encountered in the past 100 plus years, the Spanish flu, the Great Depression, dozens of recessions, Black Monday, the tech bubble bursting, the 2008/09 financial crisis, H1N1, Sars, Covid19 and so on that life insurance companies remain the most financially solvent companies in the world? No. It's an engineered outcome based on actuarial science and more than 176 years of experience. When dealing with a mutual life insurance carrier that provides dividend-paying participating whole life contracts, they are not chasing the next quarter or pressured by stockholders. They are only focused on meeting the guarantees of the contracts and supporting long-term stable dividends for their participating policy owners. They must put premium dollars to work efficiently over long periods of time to meet their contractual obligations to policy owners. And the actuaries, much like engineers, overbuild everything (a good thing for you and me).

Going back to Kim and Jack's example, the life company they co-own has the entire $10,000(PUA) to put to work and multiply. An immediate obligation of $50,000 more in total death benefit is also created, but they also understand the probability of Jack dying prematurely is very low. Yet, when each paid-up death benefit is added, the acquisition cost that the life company needs to guarantee this lifelong benefit for Jack is recovered from the premium immediately. The remainder instantly shows up as paid-up cash values for the policy owner. Constant cash accumulation begins from that day forward inside Jack's whole life policy.

The best part, Kim and Jack have ready access to more money, on-demand, on their terms. And when they borrow money from the life insurance company, using their total cash value as collateral, they essentially co-own the lender. When you co-own the lender, you'll also want to repay your loans with principal plus + interest, just like Kim and Jack do. If you own a business, would you want it to be profitable? Of course! The more profitable your business is, the more revenue-sharing potential for you as long as you own that business.

The more capital you put in, the more you get out. It is ridiculously simple!

Summary

Cash value accumulation may be a result of what happens when you purchase a paid-up addition, but the sequence of operations is the key. When you purchase a PUA, you are paying a premium that buys an immediate permanent death benefit increase. And just as the base policy must contractually grow the cash value to equal the initial starting death benefit, the same exact contract obligation is locked in for the increased PUA death benefit. The total cash value *must* equal your total death benefit value by age 100 of the life insured. Therefore, the total death benefit is ultimately what drives the growth of your total cash value—hence the title *Cash Follows the Leader*. The leader is the death benefit.

When we refer to "The Infinite Banking Concept®" or "Becoming Your Own Banker®," we are describing a ***process, not a product***. And based on our expert experience over these past fifteen (15) years+ of helping people just like you, this process is best implemented in the way that R. Nelson Nash, the developer, and creator of the concept, intended.

On the other hand, Nelson often said that dividend-paying participating whole life insurance (the product) used to implement the process is grossly misclassified.

If he could have renamed it, Nelson would refer to it as: *"A personal monetary system with a death benefit thrown in on the side for good measure."*

Correct classification of anything is important and should always be based on whatever the major characteristics are. It is clear that dividend-paying participating whole life, engineered to implement Nelson's concept, has far more financing characteristics than life insurance characteristics. He took it one step further, indicating that if you assessed your real need for financing over a lifetime and you solved this need via this product, you would have to ensure every single person an insurable interest in getting the job done.

Hence, taking control of the banking function or becoming a banker in your life requires multiple policies (a system) to finance all the things you need. It's all about building your own warehouse of wealth, an ever-increasing pool of money that never leaves your control. You set about purchasing and investing in the things you desire throughout your life while your own money (total cash value) continues growing daily, uninterrupted inside of an entity that you own and control, completely shielded from loss.

Chapter Three

Finding Money to Get Started

No treasure hunt will be required. You are already allocating one hundred (100) percent % of your financial resources to everything you've prioritized as being important. The money exists to get started. However, locating the money requires a reallocation of your priorities.

Think about periods throughout your life when you had extra money (i.e., a bonus, a gift, an unexpected windfall). What happened to all that money? Your expenses likely increased to gobble it up. You're not alone, and it's not your fault. It's happened to all of us.

What does this phenomenon tell us as your advisor? That we need to help you through a period of introspection, a real assessment of your priorities financially, including pinpointing where all the money you work hard to earn is currently flowing to.

I want you to picture the junk drawer that you have in your home right now. C'mon, you know what I'm talking about. We all have one.

It's time to dump your financial junk drawer onto the counter, sort through it all, and reprioritize.

Our team is here to help you do that.

Prior to getting started with implementing "The Infinite Banking Concept®," you must become acutely *aware* of all the money you have coming in, where it's all going, and where it is flowing to. Extra or disposable income is first in line to prioritize premium deposits. If you do not have any disposable income, it's likely because you haven't prioritized it.

And when you gain complete clarity on where all your money is flowing to, and then you reprioritize, you'll know exactly what to do. Whether it's starting your first policy, storing more money inside of an existing policy, or deciding to expand your family banking system by acquiring more policies. Either way, your financial priorities can be changed to create more wealth instead of being consumed by expenses. Money that resides inside of your system versus someone else's is money that attracts more high-caliber opportunities and stays within the family.

Think about how you currently organize and track your finances. Is it all neat and tidy or thrown into a physical "junk drawer"? Where do you keep your financial records? Is it a pile of papers or unopened envelopes? Do you have a stack of investment and bank statements where the sheer thought of opening them creates anxiety?

Some people that we meet initially cannot recite who and what they owe in debts, and no one has taken the time to help them calculate the interest volume they pay on all their debts. Interest volume ($) is not to be confused with interest rates (%). A rate is simply a percentage that is measured against an amount owed over a year. Interest volume is the actual amount of dollars that you end up paying above the principal amount borrowed. Every payment that you make is a permanent transfer of money away from you and from every generation that comes after you. You cannot use or earn interest on any of that money ever again. The lost opportunity is permanent. There are no exceptions.

That's where our team comes in. As expert coaches, we pull up a seat right next to you, and together, we thoroughly review and engage in a conversation about your financial priorities and the flow of your money. We can easily spot waste, opportunity, and danger long before our clients can. One critical element we identify for our prospective clients is their true positive cash flow. This will then initiate the process and purchase their first policy. Often, a combination of existing assets and net cash flow are combined strategically to kick-start a family or business program.

What is positive cash flow? Simply put, if you spend less than you make, you already have it. In other words, after all of your bills and expenses are paid, it's the amount of money left over. Often, when we help prospective clients sort through their financial junk drawers and clarify priorities, individuals who didn't have a positive cash flow before, find ways to create it by eliminating waste or reprioritizing where their money flows to.

For example, recently, a client shifted from being an employee to becoming a contractor in the IT space. His wife and two children had already been diligently living on the wife's income. He incorporated, and now the income he generates resides there without impacting their lifestyle. As the business owner and shareholder of the company, he controls his personal income and keeps it near zero. He had already accumulated greater than $250,000 in a registered retirement savings plan (RRSP) and grew quite dissatisfied with it.

In consultation with his accountant, he determined it made sense to begin strategically melting down these accounts now rather than pay potentially higher taxes when he needed to withdraw them at retirement. This strategy produced a new funding source for a dividend-paying participating whole life policy that created an instant tax-free death benefit amount that was needed since he had no existing life insurance coverage. This policy will also be utilized in the future as an insured retirement program. It gets better.

They had also been diligently setting aside $250 per month for each of their children inside of a registered education savings plan (RESP), funds where they lacked control and visibility. They had already maxed out the Canada Education Savings Grant (CESG) and had been accustomed to this payment in their budget for well over a decade. This same cash flow has now been directed to participating whole life insurance policies for their children, providing control and a multigenerational benefit that the whole family can use without any of the restrictions of an RESP. Then after exploring their cash flow further, it was determined they were sending weekly accelerated payments onto their mortgage.

In one phone call, they recovered $360 per week of cash flow they were happily paying to someone else's bank. Instead of building equity in their home where it was locked up, they can now build equity in their tax-exempt insurance contracts, where they have more control and peace of mind. To top it off, they had creditor insurance with their mortgage lender. They were paying $24 per week for a declining benefit that was unlikely to pay out if or when they needed it. By establishing proper insurance protection that will be there when they need it, they were able to redirect these funds also. So their cash flow was always there, but it had been allocated based on what they believed was possible at that time. Now with more education and a clear understanding of how they can work with capital for the rest of their lifetime, they were able to get their system started without working any harder, changing their cash flow, taking on any risk, and never losing control of their money. This is called working with what you've got, and you would be surprised by how practical these discovery sessions are.

https://wealthwithoutbaystreet.com/15mincall

Here is a quick summary of how this client worked with their coach to reprioritize (See the summary shown in the following chart):

- $360 + $24 = $384 per week over 52 weeks a year is $19,968 per year
- $250 x 2 Children = $500 per month. $250 redirected monthly towards a dividend-paying participating whole life policy for each child. Note - they still have the RESP's accounts, including the CESG grants, intact.
- $30,000 of voluntary RRSP reallocation per year, after the initial withholding taxes of 30%, is a net $21,000 of capital to be directed to a new cash value policy each year they choose to make this withdrawal. Being in the lowest income bracket by controlling how they earn their income made this a sensible option after discussing it with their tax professional. $9000 is withheld to pay the eventual taxes on income for that calendar year.
- Overall, four policies have been created, one for each member of the

family and roughly $47,000 annually of funding potential by adjusting where they reprioritized the "flow" of money in their life. Additionally, recognizing they wanted to be an "honest banker," they committed to depositing at minimum the same amount that used to be sent to their old retirement accounts, bringing their total up to $60,550.

- Each of their children has permanent protection greater than $110,000 to start, with guaranteed insurability options and critical illness coverage.
- The husband, who had no coverage in place prior to being introduced to our team, now has $1,000,000 in life insurance, a combination of whole life with a term rider for extra protection and conversion potential.
- The wife has $750,000 in coverage (a combination of whole life with a term rider for protection) they own and control. This is on top of the $200,000 available from her government benefit plan

Combined Deposits For The Family Banking System						
		Age 45	Age 45	Age 13	Age 9	
Parents Age	Year	CORP Policy	Wife	Child 1	Child 2	Combined
46	1	$ 30,000	$ 24,750	$ 2,900	$ 2,900	$ 60,550
47	2	$ 30,000	$ 24,750	$ 2,900	$ 2,900	$ 60,550
48	3	$ 30,000	$ 24,750	$ 2,900	$ 2,900	$ 60,550
49	4	$ 30,000	$ 24,750	$ 2,900	$ 2,900	$ 60,550
50	5	$ 30,000	$ 24,750	$ 2,900	$ 2,900	$ 60,550
51	6	$ 30,000	$ 24,750	$ 2,900	$ 2,900	$ 60,550
52	7	$ 30,000	$ 24,750	$ 2,900	$ 2,900	$ 60,550
53	8	$ 30,000	$ 24,750	$ 2,900	$ 2,900	$ 60,550
54	9	$ 30,000	$ 24,750	$ 2,800	$ 2,900	$ 60,450
55	10	$ 30,000	$ 24,750	$ 2,900	$ 2,900	$ 60,550
56	11	$ 30,000	$ 24,750	$ 2,900	$ 2,900	$ 60,550
57	12	$ 30,000	$ 24,750	$ 2,900	$ 2,900	$ 60,550
58	13	$ 30,000	$ 24,750	$ 2,900	$ 2,900	$ 60,550
59	14	$ 30,000	$ 24,750	$ 2,900	$ 2,900	$ 60,550
60	15	$ 30,000	$ 24,750	$ 2,900	$ 2,900	$ 60,550
61	16	$ 30,000	$ 24,750	$ 2,900	$ 2,900	$ 60,550
62	17	$ 30,000	$ 24,750	$ 2,900	$ 2,900	$ 60,550
63	18	$ 30,000	$ 24,750	$ 2,900	$ 2,900	$ 60,550
64	19	$ 30,000	$ 24,750	$ 2,900	$ 2,900	$ 60,550
65	20	$ 30,000	$ 24,750	$ 2,900	$ 2,900	$ 60,550
66	21	$ -	$ -	$ 2,900	$ 2,900	$ 5,800
67	22	$ -	$ -	$ 2,900	$ 2,900	$ 5,800
68	23	$ -	$ -	$ 2,900	$ 2,900	$ 5,800
69	24	$ -	$ -	$ 2,900	$ 2,900	$ 5,800
70	25	$ -	$ -	$ 2,900	$ 2,900	$ 5,800
Total Deposit Made Into The System						$ 1,239,900

They had access to cash values to work from over the whole timeframe. Focusing on passive income from age 70 to age 95, they can receive a tax-free income* to supplement their other retirement sources, as shown in the following chart.

$44,300 per year tax free income for the wife.

$33,300 per year net of tax after drawing it out of his corporation for the husband. The corporation paid all the premiums, collateralized the policy, and after issuing a dividend, this is what the shareholder can spend after taxes are paid.

If they choose, they could also access approximately $7,000 - $10,000 more per year from each of the plans they own for the lives of their children. These policies would be replenished with death benefit proceeds from the parents when they pass away, allowing the children the reuse of all that capital (plus more) for their own retirement.

This represents $92,600 a year in passive income for twenty-six years or $2,314,000 in tax-free access while they're alive using their life insurance contracts as collateral (see following chart).

Tax Free Passive Retirement Income for 26 years						
Parents Age	Year	CORP Policy	Wife	Child 1	Child 2	Combined
71	26	-$ 34,300	-$ 44,300	-$ 7,000	-$ 7,000	-$ 92,600
72	27	-$ 34,300	-$ 44,300	-$ 7,000	-$ 7,000	-$ 92,600
73	28	-$ 34,300	-$ 44,300	-$ 7,000	-$ 7,000	-$ 92,600
74	29	-$ 34,300	-$ 44,300	-$ 7,000	-$ 7,000	-$ 92,600
75	30	-$ 34,300	-$ 44,300	-$ 7,000	-$ 7,000	-$ 92,600
76	31	-$ 34,300	-$ 44,300	-$ 7,000	-$ 7,000	-$ 92,600
77	32	-$ 34,300	-$ 44,300	-$ 7,000	-$ 7,000	-$ 92,600
78	33	-$ 34,300	-$ 44,300	-$ 7,000	-$ 7,000	-$ 92,600
79	34	-$ 34,300	-$ 44,300	-$ 7,000	-$ 7,000	-$ 92,600
80	35	-$ 34,300	-$ 44,300	-$ 7,000	-$ 7,000	-$ 92,600
81	36	-$ 34,300	-$ 44,300	-$ 7,000	-$ 7,000	-$ 92,600
82	37	-$ 34,300	-$ 44,300	-$ 7,000	-$ 7,000	-$ 92,600
83	38	-$ 34,300	-$ 44,300	-$ 7,000	-$ 7,000	-$ 92,600
84	39	-$ 34,300	-$ 44,300	-$ 7,000	-$ 7,000	-$ 92,600
85	40	-$ 34,300	-$ 44,300	-$ 7,000	-$ 7,000	-$ 92,600
86	41	-$ 34,300	-$ 44,300	-$ 7,000	-$ 7,000	-$ 92,600
87	42	-$ 34,300	-$ 44,300	-$ 7,000	-$ 7,000	-$ 92,600
88	43	-$ 34,300	-$ 44,300	-$ 7,000	-$ 7,000	-$ 92,600
89	44	-$ 34,300	-$ 44,300	-$ 7,000	-$ 7,000	-$ 92,600
90	45	-$ 34,300	-$ 44,300	-$ 7,000	-$ 7,000	-$ 92,600
91	46	-$ 34,300	-$ 44,300	-$ 7,000	-$ 7,000	-$ 92,600
92	47	-$ 34,300	-$ 44,300	-$ 7,000	-$ 7,000	-$ 92,600
93	48	-$ 34,300	-$ 44,300	-$ 7,000	-$ 7,000	-$ 92,600
94	49	-$ 34,300	-$ 44,300	-$ 7,000	-$ 7,000	-$ 92,600
95	50	-$ 34,300	-$ 44,300	-$ 7,000	-$ 7,000	-$ 92,600
96	51	-$ 34,300	-$ 44,300	-$ 7,000	-$ 7,000	-$ 92,600
Total After Tax Income Used During Lifetime						-$ 2,407,600

Assuming they pass away at age ninety-six, they leave each of the kids between $500,000 and $600,000 in a tax-free windfall of death benefit proceeds. Each child can repay the $350,000 of outstanding collateral loans on their respective policies.

Now the next generation is able to pick up where the parents left off with this wealth journey. First, the kids use the net death benefit proceeds to pay off any policy loans. This replaces the full value their parents used as a passive income. Then from age 70 to 100, each of the kids can now supplement their own retirement income with $25,000 - $35,000 every year income tax-free. It is important to note that the children agreed to take over the premium deposits from the parents. In our example, the parents decided to continue funding until age 70 and then have their daughters take on this responsibility. In this family system, mom and dad are able to utilize 2.5 times more to supplement their income than they contributed to the plans on their children (see following chart).

See how the continuation of this multigenerational plan provides value up to the 91st year of setting it up. The children contributed from age 38 to age 70 for the oldest daughter and age 34 to age 70 for the youngest daughter. The oldest saved $92,800 over 32 years and the younger sister $104,400 over 36 years respectively. They each utilize more than 8.7 times what they contributed out of pocket. A legacy is created for the third generation that their grandparents started almost a century before. The net tax free death benefit is still a multiple of what each of the children deposited.

Tax Free Passive Retirement Income to age 100 of The Children				
YEAR	Child 1 Age	Child 2 Age	Child 1	Child 2
52	65	61	$ 2,900	$ 2,900
53	66	62	$ 2,900	$ 2,900
54	67	63	$ 2,900	$ 2,900
55	68	64	$ 2,900	$ 2,900
56	69	65	$ 2,900	$ 2,900
57	70	66	$ 2,900	$ 2,900
58	71	67	-$ 27,000	$ 2,900
59	72	68	-$ 27,000	$ 2,900
60	73	69	-$ 27,000	$ 2,900
61	74	70	-$ 27,000	$ 2,900
62	75	71	-$ 27,000	-$ 32,000
63	76	72	-$ 27,000	-$ 32,000
64	77	73	-$ 27,000	-$ 32,000
65	78	74	-$ 27,000	-$ 32,000
66	79	75	-$ 27,000	-$ 32,000
67	80	76	-$ 27,000	-$ 32,000
68	81	77	-$ 27,000	-$ 32,000
69	82	78	-$ 27,000	-$ 32,000
70	83	79	-$ 27,000	-$ 32,000
71	84	80	-$ 27,000	-$ 32,000
72	85	81	-$ 27,000	-$ 32,000
73	86	82	-$ 27,000	-$ 32,000
74	87	83	-$ 27,000	-$ 32,000
75	88	84	-$ 27,000	-$ 32,000
76	89	85	-$ 27,000	-$ 32,000
77	90	86	-$ 27,000	-$ 32,000
78	91	87	-$ 27,000	-$ 32,000
79	92	88	-$ 27,000	-$ 32,000
80	93	89	-$ 27,000	-$ 32,000
81	94	90	-$ 27,000	-$ 32,000
82	95	91	-$ 27,000	-$ 32,000
83	96	92	-$ 27,000	-$ 32,000
84	97	93	-$ 27,000	-$ 32,000
85	98	94	-$ 27,000	-$ 32,000
86	99	95	-$ 27,000	-$ 32,000
87	100	96	-$ 27,000	-$ 32,000
88		97		-$ 32,000
89		98		-$ 32,000
90		99		-$ 32,000
91		100		-$ 32,000
Total After Tax Income			-$ 810,000	-$ 960,000
Net Death Benefit at age 100			$ 435,000	$ 520,000

*Net death benefit based on using 80% of cash value as collateral for loans

**NOTE:

Assumptions used in this family example (on preceding page):

> *4.5% collateral loan rate (approximately 0.5% - 1.0% higher than current rates as of April 2022)
>
> *Dividends paid annually assumed at 2022 dividend scale interest rates (the lowest in 40 years)
>
> *Policy collateralized up to 90% at age 100 of the parents and 80% at age 100 for the children's retirement stage

Another client, at age 55, discovered with his coach that he could be saving on several existing insurance policies, including his home and auto, by simply changing the way in which he paid for them. He had a mixed bag of insurance policies that he could not explain to himself and his wife. In one 30-minute call, he was given some homework to call these companies and ask some very specific questions. The result was almost $2000 a year in extra cash flow that had been flowing away from his family for the last 15 years! That adds up to $30,000 of money that his family will never see, plus any earning potential along that 15-year period of time. Now with this newfound awareness, he can harness that same $2000 he was happy to give up to someone else for his own family system.

While this may not be a large sum to most, the teaching point is that we all have little inefficiencies that build up over time. A well-trained coach on our team can help you identify these and work on solutions that optimize your cash flow. So here are the steps we take when working with a prospective client:

Quick Inventory:

- Where does all your money presently flow to?
- How much money do you owe in liabilities (i.e., mortgage, car loan, credit cards, lines of credit, business loans)?
- What dollar amount do you pay in interest on your debts?
- Do you invest or save money? If so, where and how much?
- What types of existing insurance coverage do you have, and how much do you spend on that?

Now, of all the expenses you listed, how much money is leaving your pocket and going into someone else's? What if those monies were stockpiling in a warehouse you owned and controlled? How dramatically different would your life be? Think about it, and we will address it when we meet.

https://wealthwithoutbaystreet.com/15mincall

Brainstorm: Time to write down all the potential extra income events

- Bonuses
- Side hustles
- Tax refunds
- Inheritance
- Canada Child Benefit
- Expected windfall events such as the sale of a rental property, cottage, business, or inheritance
- Rental property accounts with cash flow, escrow, property tax, etc.

Isolate the Essentials: This is where you and your spouse must agree on what is truly important for your needs and what you can do without.

- Housing costs
- Food
- Utilities
- Kids activities

Tip: If you go through all your expenses and declare them all essential, go back and do it again. We guarantee that's not true.

Define Your Percentage: What percentage of your gross income is set aside for your financial advantage? This is the total sum of all voluntary payments to savings, investments, and any extra you may have sent to creditors, divided by your gross income. We recommend a bare minimum of 15%, but 25 to 30% would be optimal. If you are not in those ranges, then choose one and make it a priority. When you can apply this to a flexibly designed cash-creating machine, like a dividend-paying participating whole life policy, you will be able to collateralize a large amount of equity in a short period of time.

The Asset Summary: This is your net worth calculation. Don't panic. When we ask clients what their net worth is, many have no idea right away what they are actually worth. Basically, it's the market value of your combined assets, less what you owe at the same point in time.

Assets minus (-) Liabilities = Net Worth

Write down the market value of your assets (what you could sell them for today). Include everything you can think of, such as

- Value of real estate holdings.
- Business accounts and business valuation (assuming you would be able to sell it).
- Investment & savings accounts (TFSA, RRSPs, LIRA's, and RESPs are included).
- Cryptocurrencies, bullion, collectibles (that could be turned into cash).
- Deduct the costs to transition that asset into cash, such as real estate fees, taxes, legal expenses, etc.
- Circle or highlight those highly liquid assets. These are the assets you could turn into cash within 30-45 days.
- Write down all the debts you have. Include any private loans you have with family members and taxes owed to Canada Revenue Agency (CRA).
- Then take the amounts of the above points and subtract the liabilities from your asset valuation, and you have your net worth.

Summary

When you map out where one hundred percent (100%) of your financial resources are already being allocated, you will find the money to get started.

An advisor on our team can help you move forward and reach your goal of Becoming Your Own Banker®. Honesty, clarity, and the desire to change are *the* critical elements for this process to be effective for you.

Chapter Four

The Financial Mini-Van

So, once you've got complete clarity on your financial position and the amount of your positive cash flow, assuming you have some or found a way to create it for yourself, what's next? I hear many say, "Well, we will just invest it into the stock market or stash it away in our savings account." Hmmm, do we think that makes sense? No, and by now, you know that we will say none of those options is a guaranteed way to create wealth. And neither will allow you to become your own banker.

A question we like to ask in this circumstance is: What do a Vegas casino and a supercar have in common? They are all flash and have no substance. Sure, they are fun for short spurts, but they are not steady and consistent. How many times have you been to a casino and won big? How many times have you lost big? And if you've ever driven a sports car like a Lamborghini or Bugatti, how did it handle the long haul? Would you use it as your daily driver to take the kids to school, shop, or transport the family dog? Not to mention the additional time and costs associated with custom parts and service needs!

Why do we ask you this? Well, because the concept of a casino or supercar deals in short-term fun and highs, not long-term gains and consistency. The same holds true in how you choose your financial vehicles. Think about it, there is always the sexy new product being promoted as the next best thing: "Get in on the ground floor!" "This will make you richer than your wildest dreams!" But the truth is those cavalier, overly embellished statements are nothing short of an unrealistic promise to fulfill your dreams and fantasies, just like the thought of pulling up to the Bellagio hotel in Vegas in a Bugatti Veran.

The stock markets shift through cycles. If you read our first book, you will recall our discussion on the crash of 2008, where half the globe was impacted. Eventually, the markets slowly rebounded, and we have since experienced a bull market for most of the last ten years (up to early 2022). As the rebound began, all the gurus came out of the woodwork, professing they had the answers to getting back on track and taking a piece of the upswing. We liken it to getting on a rollercoaster after it starts to move. It's all about as pointless as buying a lottery ticket, hoping you will win so you can retire. It's gambling, pure and simple.

On May 12, 2022, a CNN article noted that more than $7 trillion worth of value had been wiped out of the stock market in the first half of 2022. Even Netflix, something that has become a consumer staple and a globally recognized company, was down over 70% from its peak. The article notes that the Nasdaq was down 27% overall, and the other stock indexes were not fairing much better. It's interesting to see Netflix experiencing a surprise turnaround similar to the demise of Blockbuster, which filed for bankruptcy in 2010. Who's to say what the future holds for this streaming service but the safety and peace of mind that comes with the guaranteed growth, as your cash follows the leader with your whole life insurance, is a stark contrast.

Let's go back to the sports car analogy. There is a reason that supercars are not recommended as family vehicles. They aren't built with the features to accommodate the needs of a family. There is little seating, no room for storage or car seats, safety concerns, and they may not be very dependable. They are high-cost, exciting to drive, and look cool, but they won't perform the core functions the way you likely need them to, and that's the kicker.

So, as you look at your financial life and contemplate what vehicle to use, do you want speed and all the potential risks it comes with, or do you want flexibility, longevity, and a guaranteed producer? If you answer that question the same way you think about family, you might have less financial stress throughout your life. Remember the story of the tortoise and the hare. Who won the race? Right, the tortoise because slow and steady wins every time. And that vehicle is the dividend-paying whole life policy or, as we call it, the financial minivan.

Summary

The minivan may not reach top speeds or turn heads, but it is competitive with most vehicles on the road today. It accounts for all your family; it's safe, diverse in its amenities, and reliable. With your hands firmly planted on the wheel of the financial minivan, you can accomplish every financial objective you want by taking it to exactly where you want to go. It becomes the foundation from which all other financial decisions you must tackle begin. Like a family road trip filled with memories, your generational legacy will be realized if you engage and teach your children and grandchildren to embrace this mindset of Becoming Your Own Banker® while using your financial minivan or whole life policy. You will start to think and act intergenerationally and prosper as a family in the same way the large banking families like the Rockefellers and the Rothschilds have done.

Chapter Five

Why Diversify in Lives/ Next Steps

We've all heard the saying, don't put all your eggs in one basket. Well, if you control the basket, how many of your eggs do you not want in it? If you're familiar with the buzzword "diversification," you can hang around with the folks on wall street or bay street. The reason or rationale for "diversification" is to prevent you from losing all of your money in any one investment. The thinking is that the more you divide your "nest egg" into different financial vehicles or companies, the better chance you have of the good outweighing the bad and, therefore, a steadier growth. The hope is that you reduce overall risk by having more winners than losers in a given year and, over time, on your combined portfolio.

To some, it translates into, "Don't bother learning too much about one specific industry or sector. You can just put on a blindfold and throw darts at your financial dartboard." We clearly do not subscribe to this way of thinking because it's nothing more than a wish, a hope, and a prayer that everything turns out ok.

What is the alternative? One way requires a bit more education and analysis on the part of the investor. You would have to research companies, trends, and the economy to make informed decisions about where to invest your money. This is true investing. The former method is nothing but pure speculation. For example, a real estate investor might zone in on a particular city and neighborhood because of the job market trend and major infrastructure improvements taking place versus buying in a location they know absolutely nothing about. Nelson Nash used to say, ***"...an investment should only be in something you know a great deal about...everything else is speculation!"*** However, speculation is much more the norm—most confuse speculation with investing.

There is equal confusion when it comes to defining capital. Our friend and Austrian economist, Ryan D. Griggs, is the best one to explain what capital is. Griggs defines capital as the "...abstract, hypothetical, typically subjective monetary value of an asset." Basically, whatever you can realize in net currency when selling something is its capital valuation. For example, your home may be considered an asset, but the net equity you could receive if it was sold is its capital. This value can shift year to year based on market conditions. Whereas, with a par whole life policy, capital is clear, consistent, and constantly growing by virtue of the contract it is built on. Providing access to capital is the foundation of the banking business. By capitalizing your own system, you create access to a capital pool from the life company you co-own while preserving your own capital assets principle, the cash value. This is the power of leverage combined with the maximum amount of control, a banker's dream!

Capital provides more control and, by its nature, is not speculative. Without access to a liquid pile of capital, opportunities that show up in our lives cannot be funded. Ask yourself, is there any such thing as having too much capital? Have you ever heard of a business failing because it was "over-capitalized"? Of course not! Therefore, if you want to take advantage of an opportunity, your options are directly correlated to the size of the capital pool you can access. Whose capital pile do you want to tap into? A 3rd party gatekeeper, such as a commercial bank or finance company, or the pile you have exclusive control over at a company you co-own with mutual whole life insurance? Griggs indicates that Nelson's Infinite Banking Concept is, simply put, ***"the best way to systematically accumulate and optimally deploy capital over a lifetime."***

To learn more about capital, access our interview with Ryan Griggs here: **wealthwithoutbaystreet.com/capitaltheory**

Systematic accumulation of capital via monthly or annual premium deposits will create a solid financial foundation. From this base of operation, you can now effectively and with newfound confidence begin deploying capital as you need, such as pouncing on strategic opportunities and big deals. Many of our clients begin by taking control of the banking function as it relates to their household or business needs. This involves reclaiming 3rd party debts from other lending institutions into your control, using policy loans. Then commit that stream of payments to your own system so you never again lose control over that precious cash flow. This can rapidly increase your capital base and naturally leads to acquiring the actual investments you seek out, with educated intent, from your capital warehouse.

By capital warehouse, we, of course, are referring to many participating whole life policies where you have available funds built into your "cash values" to borrow against. With the power of this collateral, you can take policy loans and acquire the things you need in life and pounce on high-caliber opportunities. So, when we use the title like diversify in bodies, we refer to the lives you insure to accumulate multiple policies. Each policy created, if maintained by the policy owner, will efficiently grow, day in and day out, with cash values chasing after a growing death benefit until the day the insured person is no longer with us. At that point, a tax-free cheque is cut to the named beneficiaries as chosen by the policy owner, who maintains control of the whole system.

Remember, in chapter one, R. Nelson Nash at one time had 49 life insurance policies on himself, family members, and former business partners. In fact, Nelson started five policies on business partners. He experienced not just one but two death claims on ex-business partners whom he did not even associate with any longer after their partnership projects were long finished. Now, the remaining three policies will still pay a tax-free benefit to Nelson's heirs as he was able to decide the contingent owner of these assets before he passed away. Much like Nelson acquired very strategic real estate investments using policy loans during his life, the new policy owner can do the same thing now that they control this rising daily asset.

We practice what we preach and follow Nelson's good guidance. Success leaves clues; we simply mirror and model the system that has worked so well for Nelson and his family. We each own multiple policies in our own lives and that of our family members, as indicated in chapter one. On top of that, we are focused on starting additional ones as soon as we can envision adding another. Our families have control over all the cash values that accumulate. These multiple policies create the growing pool of financial value we need to build wealth and mitigate risk for everyone participating in the family banking system. It allows for seamless continuity and the ripple effect to carry the system forward through generations.

And remember, when Nelson passed away in March 2019, seventeen death benefit cheques were paid tax-free. In addition, 28 policy contracts on different insured people that Nelson started are still in force after he graduated. This means that 28 cash-accumulating assets continue to grow the Nash family capital base as they follow the leader of the growing death benefits.

Nelson's children experienced what he referred to as a "windfall" event. Where large chunks of money come in at unexpected times. They were able to use this money to replenish outstanding policy loans on their own system and consider starting new policies. There is also significant participating whole life coverage of Mary Nash; eventually, another windfall event will occur upon her graduation. This all took place despite the many ups and downs of market cycles over the 88 years of Nelson's life.

Powerful stuff, right?

Now, some may find this fact morbid, but we can assure you that there are two sure things in this world: death and taxes. And the only thing that doesn't get worse each time politicians meet is death. We can plan for both but can't prevent either. By arranging for death, using the most effective life insurance tool on the planet, a very positive ripple effect begins to occur:

- You can sleep easier, knowing both you and those you love are protected.
- You become the co-owner of a company that is legally bound to grow a pool of accessible financial value every single day until the life insured passes away, at which time a death benefit is paid.
- You control access to money as the policy owner, no matter who the

life-insured person is, by using the policy as collateral. These funds can be used to invest in a business, education, real estate, or anything else you desire.

- You can essentially "live" the death benefit while alive, as can the other bodies you insure if you implement the strategies we teach you, to truly embrace family banking.
- You can reduce your overall lifetime tax bill because the growth of each policy is tax-exempt. In addition to that, by working with an advisor on our team, you can learn how to access tax-free capital to supplement and, in many cases, even replace a retirement income altogether.
- You set the stage for the 3rd or 4th generation to participate in this process.
- When death comes, and it will come, the system becomes self-sustaining.
- You adjust your monthly and annual spending patterns to prioritize paying yourself first, systematically, with your premium deposits.
- You will have a heightened awareness of opportunities and the liquidity and ability to act on them.
- You join an elite class of Canadians in our community that is changing the way they think and act intergenerationally with more financial control.

If all you did was to ensure every person you love and those you have an insurable interest in, then re-allocated the cash flow you are currently spending to well-designed participating whole-life policies, you would automatically achieve uninterrupted growth in a tax-advantaged environment.

Now, at some point, you will lose a loved one, or your loved ones will lose you. It is unavoidable. Rather than be a statistic, your family is positioned to be a success story, just like the Rockefellers. Jayson is fond of quoting the late Ben Feldman, who said: ***"the best definition of an investment is the one that pays the most when you need it the most."*** Think about it. Tax-free proceeds that show up in our time of need will provide the remaining family members time to grieve, the space to make good decisions, and the resources to go on living.

Now, suppose you did more speculation than our recommended method. What would happen in the event of your death? In Canada, all of your capital property is deemed to have been disposed of (or sold) at fair market value at the moment of your death. These assets could include investment accounts, the shares in any business you own, your cottage at the lake, rental properties, and even your tax-qualified plans such as RRSPs. That's right, everything you own is assessed at the fair market value at the moment of your death. Your date of death becomes the basis for tax calculation.

Would you believe it? The Canadian Revenue Agency (CRA) has no sense of humor at all when it comes to this, and they won't accept any substitutes for money, such as the shares in your corporation, stamp collections, a rental property, or your classic corvette to pay the tax bill. That means your heirs will now have to pay the final tax bill in Canadian currency. For many Canadians, this means liquidation.

Everything you spent a lifetime building gets torn down at a discount price as your executor is forced to sell things off to pay the final tax bill. What if your investment accounts have dropped in value substantially from the moment of your death to when the terminal tax return is filed? It doesn't matter. The tax bill will be derived from the fair market value of all your capital property. If your stock portfolio was purchased with $500,000, the fair market value was $1,000,000 at the moment of your death and dropped to $400,000 at the time that your terminal tax return was filed, your loved ones will be subject to pay tax on the $500,000 capital gain, versus a $100,000 capital loss. Speculation will never give you the peace of mind of being your own banker will. But knowing that all you have *will* be given to those you love, tax-free, and they won't have to sell at a discount, everything you have worked so hard for, that is true peace of mind.

Does this give you a new perspective? It should!

Summary

What did your parents always say, "more isn't always better?" Well, with the Infinite Banking concept®, it can be. The more warehouses of capital you can create, the more control and flexibility you build into your financial life. And when you gain more control of the money that flows through your life, building on it like a Lego tower—your base policy and the flexible paid-up additions premiums will be how you fund your life for homes, cars, education, and investments (true investments, not speculative). Embrace this new process with intentionality, and you will find the peaceful, stress-free financial way of life you seek! And we'll be right alongside you to help.

Join us, and let's get you the financial life that you deserve.

Your next action is very simple. Have a conversation with us with one of our expert coaches today.

https://wealthwithoutbaystreet.com/15mincall

Once you schedule a conversation, you will want to be ready for the call. The best way to prepare is to follow our seven-step guide to Becoming Your Own Banker®. Download the guide for free by going to 7steps.ca. This will show you the exact learning path necessary to become successful in this process. The more you continue your path of education with the Infinite Banking concept®, the more you will see that you did not see before. Thousands can attest to it!

References

"Abstract, hypothetical, typically subjective monetary value of an asset.", Ryan D. Griggs. Why Nelson is an Heir to Menger 2019 Nelson Nash Think Tank Lecture. Retrieved from: https://www.youtube.com/watch?v=o0dKTuY6Bwc&

https://ryandgriggs.medium.com/financial-philistine-dave-ramsey-attacks-the-infinite-banking-concept-again-fe1f050e4f9e

Nash, Nelson (2003, January 1). Becoming Your Own Banker 6th ed.: Infinite Banking Concepts.

La Monica, Paul R (2022, May 12). More than $7 trillion has been wiped out from the stock market this year. Retrieved from https://www.cnn.com/2022/05/12/investing/stocks-bear-market/index.html

Notes:

Made in United States
Orlando, FL
01 February 2025

58042351R00046